BEAR and the CASTLE

The James Oliver Curwood Story

by Inez Ross

For Elizabeth with best wishes July 1, 2000 Mackinaw

Inez Ross

Ashley House

Copyright 1997 by Inez Ross

All rights reserved, including the right to reproduce this book or portion thereof in any form.

Published by Ashley House
614 47th St.
Los Alamos, New Mexico

ISBN 0-9664337-0-X
Library of Congress Card Number 98-92975

Photos courtesy of
Ivan Conger
Shiawassee County Historical Society
and Inez Ross

Digital Assistance by S. Gunn

Thanks to
Nicholas Whalen who posed as young James
and to Lois Whalen as the school teacher

For
Lois and Lynette

Books by Inez Ross

The Strange Disappearance of
Uncle Dudley: A Child's Story of Los Alamos

The Adobe Castle
A Southwest Gothic Romance

The Bear and the Castle
The James Oliver Curwood Story

Way back in the eighteen hundreds a boy named Jimmy lived on a farm in Ohio with his parents, two sisters and a brother.

They were quite poor and the land was rocky. Jimmy had to help pick up rocks to clear the fields.

Timothy James Whalen II
(grandson of Lois + James Whalen)

Nicholas James Whalen son of Randy Whalen & grandson of James & Lois Whalen

Jimmy went to a one-room school. He learned to read and write.

To Dear Liz, Please visit Jim & Lois Whalen
1433 S. Pearce St.
Owosso, MI 48867
1-989-725-7516
cell 277-8917

Lois Whalen (sister of author, Inez Ross)
We are the Ashley Sisters!

His teacher showed him interesting stories in books. He liked stories of adventure.

4

As soon as he could write, he used his imagination to make up stories himself.

He imagined great adventures and made up stories of Indians, pirates, and castles.

Jimmy loved the out-of-doors. He went hunting and fishing.

He dreamed of being a great hunter when he grew up.

OWOSSO
Michigan

When he was a teenager, the family moved back to Owosso, Michigan.

Owosso was the town where Jimmy was born. He saw the building which was his birthplace.

He kept writing and when he was sixteen, two of his stories were published. Now he was a real author.

Later he signed his name James Oliver Curwood. His favorite pastimes were writing and hunting and fishing in the wilderness.

He loved to swim and fish in the Shiawassee River at Owosso and in the rivers of the North.

He married a lady named Ethel who also loved nature and camping in the wilderness.

James built hunting cabins in the forest and liked to write in them.

He used his own experiences and his imagination to write books of adventure.

He became a scout for the Canadian government and made trips into the northern territories.

In those days there were no game limits. James enjoyed shooting as many bears as he could each season.

19

On one hunting trip he went looking for a huge bear.

The bear was big enough to be called the Grizzly King.

He imagined how big a rug the bear would be if he killed him. But even though he wounded the bear, it got away.

As he was following the bear up onto a high ledge, he fell and broke his gun.

The bear turned back
and had him trapped
on the ledge!

The bear growled and looked down at him. Then surprisingly the huge animal turned and walked away. His life had been spared!

His escape gave him more respect for the wild animals. He came to believe, like his Indian friends, that hunters should shoot only as much as they needed to eat.

Many native American decendants still reside in Owosso & Chesaning MI.

James became a conservationist. He worked to protect the animals and the trees and to clean up the rivers.

He wrote the story of his experience with the bear in a book called The Grizzly King.

Later the story was made into a motion picture called The Bear.

On the banks of the Shiawassee River he built a castle like the ones he had seen in France.

Castles are symbols of romantic adventure, and James used his castle as a writing studio where he composed more stories.

Today in Owosso you can visit the castle which is a James Oliver Curwood museum.

In the great hall there are Curwood books and paintings showing scenes from the novels.

In the main tower of the castle you can see movie posters advertising Curwood films.

You can also see the actual typewriter he used to write his stories.

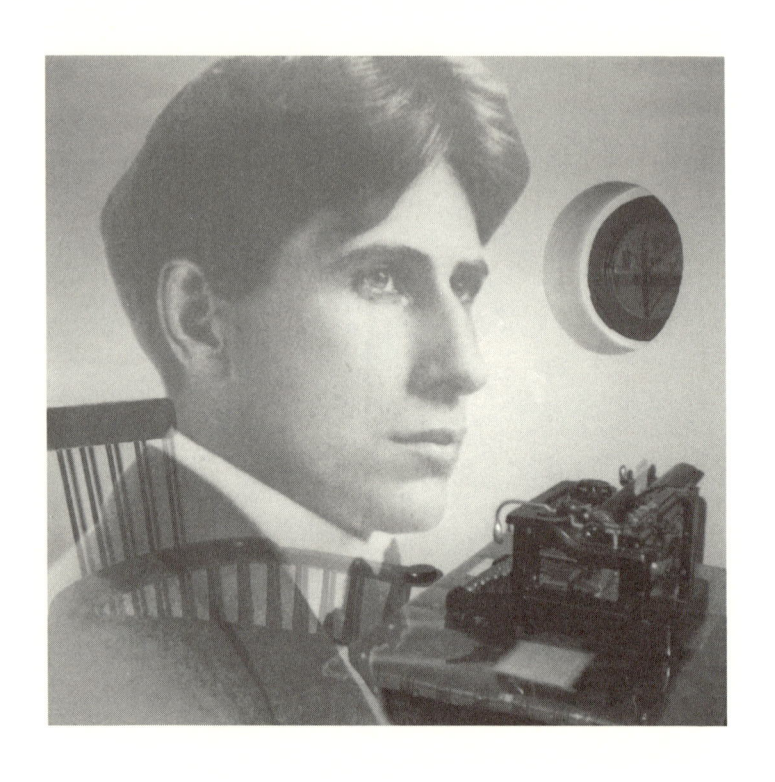

We can imagine, as James did, the outdoors and the animals as he wrote.

37

In addition to the short stories and screen plays, he wrote thirty-three books.

He became the famous conservationist and author whose stories entertain us and stir our imagination.

39

Owosso will always remember the young boy who dreamed of being a great hunter and writer. Each June the city of Owosso pays tribute to him with Curwood Days.

Curwood films are shown, festive banners decorate the streets, and thousands of visitors enjoy parades and fun on the Shiawassee River. They also learn much more about the Castle and the man responsible for it-James Oliver Curwood.

"Nature is my religion. It is my desire and my ambition to take my readers with me into the heart of this nature. I love it and I feel that they must love it ... if only I can get the two acquainted."

-James Oliver Curwood

The Books of James Oliver Curwood

1908	The Courage of Captain Plum
1908	The Wolf Hunters
1909	The Great Lakes
1909	The Gold Hunters
1910	The Danger Trail
1911	The Honor of the Big Snows
1911	Philip Steele (Steele of the Royal Mounted)
1912	The Flower of the North
1913	Isobel
1914	Kazan
1915	God's Country and the Woman
1916	The Hunted Woman
1916	The Grizzly King
1917	Baree, Son of Kazan
1918	The Courage of Marge O'Doone
1919	Nomads of the North
1919	The River's End
1920	Back to God's Country
1920	The Valley of Silent Men
1921	God's Country - The Trail to Happiness
1921	The Golden Snare
1921	The Flaming Forest
1922	The Country Beyond
1923	The Alaskan
1924	A Gentleman of Courage
1925	The Ancient Highway
1926	Swift Lightning
1926	The Black Hunter
1928	The Plains of Abraham
1929	The Cripple Lady of Peribonka
1930	Green Timber
1930	Son of the Forest (Autobiography)
1931	Falkner of the Inland Seas